The Yin Yang of Yo Yos

The Yin Yang of Yo Yos

Dr. Kurteous Kitsch

iUniverse, Inc.
New York   Bloomington

The Yin Yang of Yo Yos

iUniverse books may be ordered through booksellers or by contacting:

iUniverse
1663 Liberty Drive
Bloomington, IN 47403
www.iuniverse.com
1-800-Authors (1-800-288-4677)

Because of the dynamic nature of the Internet, any Web addresses or links contained in this book may have changed since publication and may no longer be valid.

ISBN: 978-1-4502-0386-9 (sc)
ISBN: 978-1-4502-0387-6 (ebk)

Printed in the United States of America

iUniverse rev. date: 01/11/2010

Foreword

I never really ever thought myself as a writer. I still don't know if I'm a writer. I guess I just like putting words together to create a visual scene. Now, I'm a painter, and I understand the symbols used in this artistic language, but a writer? I will let you be the judge.

Writing has always been a way for me to express my overworked imagination. I remember as a kid I loved to write. I wrote about the life of a penny when I was in sixth grade. The story was about a penny that traveled the world. I wrote a poem in seventh grade about mankind being held responsible for their actions by a committee of aliens from outer space. I even wrote a short story in college about my grandfather's pop bottle glasses. However, at the time, I never thought my writing was equal to my painting, drawing, sculpture, or mixed-media arts. It wasn't until I found out that I had a health condition called fibromyaglia that I started to use this medium as a creative voice.

This collection of writing spans twenty-five years of my life. I write now out of artistic preference. Words for me are so to the point. They can be created as I sit in my pajamas in front of a keyboard or with a notebook and pen. I don't have to wait for the idea to dry. If I don't like what I wrote, I just hit delete.

I wish life could be like this. Writing has become a way for me to express without really any preparation. *The Yin Yang of Yo Yos* is a collection of eclectic thoughts, visions, dreams, and talks to myself. I really can't tell you what the theme is, for it changes like the wind. What I can tell you is *The Yin Yang of Yo Yos* made me put my life in order, and this was no easy feat. I found that I have rediscovered myself, and this was a great awakening. So, without any more explanation, I'll get right to it. Enjoy.

Dr. Kurteous Kitsch

This collection of work came from a spiritual crisis I was having. In short, I thought God had forgotten about little old me. I know this makes no sense, but we all need some self-pity now and then. I sat down and started writing. The following writings are called "The God Series." I wrote as if God and I were hanging out with each other. These writings took on a life of their own. What started as me writing to God turned into me and God in movies, stories, and life events.

I Wrote God a Letter Today

I thought as I awoke I needed to speak to my life
It had to be on the best stationery
how would I address it
God knows me
So I decided to draw God a picture
It would be on the best paper
What would I draw
God knows how everything looks
So I decided I would sing
I don't sing very well
I decided I really had lost my way to talk with God
What if I kept a secret
Just between me and God
But God knows all my secrets
I decided to go and find God
yes find God
Because God is everything
It would take me my lifetime to find God
I decided this journey would be the God

God Wrote Me Back

Juggling groceries as I came home from my morning routine
My breath stilled me
by the mailbox
I just opened it and grabbed all the contents
I put the bags on the wobbling kitchen table
needed my sight
lost bifocals
one piece of mail
airborne to the floor
I didn't need my outer vision to see it
whiter than the purest snow
I knelt and looked at the crispness of it
It was addressed to me
The deep midnight ink
Sender God
I opened the voice of the letter
Dearest soul
answers and questions
Where to begin
As Glinda said
Always best to start at the beginning
Well there was never one or an end
People think too much
They love the freewill chance
I'm asked to cure all that is wrong
Why should I
I gave creation to creation
People need to discover themselves
The divine soul is the map
Don't try to read it
experience it
Let your soul think
Not the mind

don't use logic
become logic
don't use
use
just be
simple

A Postcard from God

It arrived with the usual postal stripes
the front was a single star engulfed
by its own darkness
hello from your higher vision
the **four corners** ripped
just
a little
message
eternity needs more light
I looked at the lone star on the front
the heavens looked as a 3 in the morning bedroom doorway
more light
maybe we need some more insight

Breakfast with God

another pink pack dissolves into eternity
the orthopedic shoe lady stood there with a pencil and pad
I'll have the veggie omelet
In my mind words spoke
see I eat healthy
He spoke
Just as the morning sun cast a ray of light across him

A bowl of Lucky Charms
the orthopedic lady scribbled and limped away
more coffee more pink packages
the orthopedic lady returned
my veggie omelet full of grease
there was a bowl of Lucky Charms
I looked I didn't see the usual half-deformed marshmallow
shapes
I saw a beautiful earth shaped one
the sun one was stunning
However Saturn was a precious detailed of fine art
all the planets crafted with such perfection
spoon in mouth
some milk dripping down his left cheek

Coffee with God

God opened two of the pink packages
sprinkled holy into the blackness
sweetened the unknown depths of a darkened thought
I said that will give you cancer
he sipped on the evergreen-trimmed diner cup
no he said
you give yourself cancer
I went for the real stuff and the cream
watching the cream glaze over the blackness
this must be hell
a clearing of his throat made me in time
he leaned forward
I looked into his eyes
fear struck me
I knew why
I saw my own reflection

Riding the Bus with God

I knew it was going to be a long bus ride
and he had the window seat
you know I said you're the one with a view
while I'm stuck with the large lady's love ass in my face
can we switch seats so I can see I asked
he said no I like the window seat
oh please I said you can see everything that ever was is and
going to be
I'm just asking to switch seats
you know I said Cecil DeMille should have shown the truth
about you in the movie
please the *Ten Commandments* what sugar-coated reality
I do like the music from it
he looked at me
did that win an Oscar
I laughed
I have forgotten how he can make me laugh at times
I liked you better as George Burns
he was sippin' his Dunkin' Donuts coffee
the multicolored hair Xanax woman behind us
engulfing one whole seat
we could hear her headset
"I'm on a highway to hell" echoed
sippin' his coffee he asked if that song ever won an award
I don't know I said as little red dot children leaned into me
still sippin' his Dunkin'
he took my hand and whispered
you know there is no such place as hell
I rolled my eyes
and what about the pearly gates
he reached up and pulled the stop signal
he stepped off the bus
of course using the rear door

waved good-bye
I scooted over to the window seat
looking at things going by
it all became a carnival
his carnival

Playing Putt-Putt Golf with God

I stood there spooning my frozen super-size cherry slurpy
He stood there watching the windmill arms go around
It was his swing
He turned and asked me to be quiet
Oh come on I said
You can stop time
But you can't get the ball between the windmill's arms
He said as he looked at me
egos
Why did I create them
and
Sarcasm
that's another story
The family following us were devoted putt-putters
They were all dressed alike in a golfer's fashion
I said you are holding up a lot of people here
The Sandcastle one is next
That's the one where if you miss you're swinging in a foot of
water
but you can always divide it
He was intently observant
But I'm the one with the cherry slurpy
and winning
He made the swing
smack
right into the windmill

I laughed
He said this is how he felt when he did the big bang thing
It's just a game I said sippin' my watered-down slurpy
It's all a game he said
and all games must end
With that he took his second swing
The ball glided on angel wings right through the windmill's
doorway
He smiled

Me and God Meet the *Wizard of Oz*

Was it a dream was it for real
I don't know or even care
All I remember was as I opened my bedroom door
I was engulfed in earth tones
I was there watching Judy!!!!
as she had basket in hand
Toto in her arm ready to open the front door
I looked at my clothes **3** times
My wholeness was in colors of the grain of dust
Judy! Judy! I cried
I could not be heard
She opened the
door
The color crept across the floor like a metaphysical mist
Colors of all colors as on a paintbrush stroked my soul
I followed behind her as she took that famous film history
step
I watched as color breathed onto both of us
I knew he was here and I owed him
He was one of the munchkins
As these little people danced
He came over to me

I was standing in the very spot where the wicked witch was
going to make her scene
He spoke in a high-pitched voice
Is this your dreams of dreams he asked I looked down at him
He was the mayor
I said I can die now and go to heaven
He said look around, you might be there already
From a far came the pink glorious bubble
Over my head as a halo it floated
Pink became my aura
Living is what you are doing now I thought
Not stuck in that way of living you called life
He said
How does it feel to be in a film actually alive
You are going on a journey with
Music
Flying Monkeys
Wicked Witches

3
Best friends
I looked at him
He had become a lollipop boy
He said use your
HEART
MIND
COURAGE
Oh and do have enough sense to move
Because houses do get dropped on people
Just then I remembered the
SLIPPERS
By now Margaret Hamilton was watching them disappear
from her sister's feet
What a great gift he had given me
My heaven on earth

And I would pay attention to the
MAN
behind the curtain

Me and God Meet "Puff the Magic Dragon"

Imagination lived by the sea
Lived in a memory
In a land called
HONALEE

kites and giant rings
make room
FOR A FAITH BECOMING LOST
A Faith needing answers
A Faith not happy
A Faith not remembered
A Faith of little Jackie Paper

Melodies rang through my head
This song **MIRRORED**
My childhood
Reflected my adulthood
Why I ask him
Must we
GROW
UP
leaving all our imagination in torn wet cardboard boxes
in some corner of a forgotten house

To hold to this innocence would be a song of **HOPE**
This could end
VIOLENCE
WAR
HATRED

He hummed the song
Spoke the words
Turned the leaves to autumn
He frolicked

Why can't I stay here I asked
He sighed
He spoke
Just listen to the song
THE WORDS
Then one day it happened
He said again
You
Choose

Me and God Meet van Gogh

His eyes did shine of blue
As he sketched the trees
As he took his
OWN
Life

I stood there listening to the wind
It became Vincent's
VOICE
The clouds passing over the stars
STARRY STARRY NIGHT
All this in my sight
My soul danced with delight

The moon shined of a yellow
STROKE
Stillness
For this creative soul

van Gogh
I
Asked
Why could you not grow old
I had to ask him
Why
HIS
LIFE
Was
Lived so short

I didn't have to look for him
He was each stroke placed throughout
VINCENT'S
LIFE
Still I had to ask him
Could you have not saved him
Think of what great pieces of art he could have
CREATED
You let him kill his
Soul
Justice you say
As free will is done

We miss him
I
Miss him
Vincent interrupted
He
Did save me
He gave me the greatest
GIFT
Just as he did for you
A moment in
Time
To make something happen

Be it
GREAT
Or
Small

I
Took my life
But
DEATH
Is not the end
Each has a
STARRY STARRY NIGHT
TO LIVE AND TO
Defend

Me and God Meet *Willy Wonka*

I have been on a celluloid cloud lately
I was letting some M&Ms melt
Just relaxing
Eyes closed
Ompa-Lompa Ompity-Da
I open my eyes
I hear Gene Wilder singing
PURE IMAGINATION
I am face down on Easter basket grass
Mint is what I taste
The Buttercups are very good
They taste like fried carnival waffle wheels
Sprinkled with powderd sugar
I stand in time to see the fat boy fall into the chocolate river
I listened
If you want to view paradise
Simply

Look
Around
And view it
Tears softly rolling down my cheek
How true
How true
I
THOUGHT
I had found him
It wasn't like the other times we spoke
There was no talking to him as some
PERSONIFICATION
Listening to
If **YOU** want to view paradise
Just simply look around and view it
I had found him
Now we want to go see
VIOLET
TURN
BLUEBERRY

Me and God in the *Sound of Music*

How do you solve a problem like Maria
The panoramic turning of the Austrian alps
Such an innocent faith singing
The hills are alive with the sound of music
The sound of his voice
The echo of his humming
The resounding hymn of his sneeze
The von Trapp family singers
One is my namesake
I want to stay riding the bicycles
Singing doe a deer a female deer

All this to be smothered
With the reason of a red-and-blackened hate
Triumph of climbing every mountain
I knew he was there
The voice of reason
He wasn't in the ornate
He wasn't in the hills
Or the sound of the hills
He was the thought
Of the simple song
Climb every mountain
He never spoke to me in this vision
It was a game of hide 'n' seek
It is the game we call life
In our stillness
Searching for a dream

Me and God in *Green Acres*

Da Da Da Da dum dum
Da Da Da Da dum dum
Green Acres is the place to
BE
Faith of ***GOD*** in a country that used to be
Purple mountain so reigning high
KEEP
Washington DC
Just give me my **SPIRIT** pride

CAPITALISM
Is where I want to be
Policing the **WORLD** telling all how to be free
Thank you
GEORGE BUSH

You are a miracle want to be
Keep religion far from
ME

Da Da Da Da dum dum
Da Da Da dum dum

But this is my life
Green acres I will always be here
Salt of the earth so
DEAR

Me and God in the Attic with Anne Frank

I found myself in the stillness of dust
The room colored in a pale confederate blue
The window is where *I* awakened
There *I* stood as the young JEWISH **girl** had
The sunlight filtered through the time full etched glass
Standing there while my eyes danced off of the golden
CHURCH BELLS
The leaning tree still witnessed to what happened
Here
Self-Sanctuary
My face started to redden with a heat glow
I did not see him
AND
I did not want to
My mind in
Anger
My soul so
Hateful
To
HIM

Why did you let this happen
Innocence killed by the marching metal
The flag of red with black
HATE SIGNED

The church bells started to ring
I was here as it was happening

SCREAMS
Vibrating my soul
Even more
HATE
For him
The footsteps echoed
Doors slammed
WHY
GOD
Did you let this happen
I raged
My faith had been stolen

The church bells rang
A spring wind cooled the heat of my fiery face
I could not move
I turned as a gust of reasoning or faith
Flowed onto me

TORN
Pieces of life on paper
Flying around me as
ANGELS
I grasped at one
Looked at it
Church bells ringing
I read
DEAR DIARY
Today I know that

LOVE
Is with in all people
It became my **FAITH**
Again
I had found him

The next body of work is inspired by my faith in God. I must admit faith in God is a life process. I know my own faith has changed over the years, from my younger days, when I was taught to fear him, to my philosophical days to question him. I never feel God would oppose me questioning his existence. I trust him and know there is a greatness that I cannot rationalize, even though I was raised to spell his name with three simple letters G-O-D.

The Metaphysical Movie Man's Machine

Theme songs from *Chitty Chitty Bang Bang*
World ending with rabbit ears judging
Static and Static
Abstract pictures of emotions
Faith
Only
Faith endures
A simulated mahogany box
Clear
Clear
Cloudy
Cloudy
Colorful
Colorful
Souls commercial
The creation of man
Operates on AA batteries
Glitter
Our emotions
Be
Gone

You have
No power
Power
Here

The Wind of Life

Clouds passing
As I lay on the deepen green summer grass
I know the age of my soul is passing
By
All the answers I have
Only a faith can answer
This is mirrored
By
Who I call myself
These clouds
Are
Creation in prayer
If creation finds faith
I know my meaning is …

Genesis a Go Go

All time glittering and guessing
Sparkles of the sea
In the grotto of faith
Time at a standstill
Party of the holy trinity
Glinda and Jesus are dating
Donation
One sand dollar

Mother's Musical Box

Enshrined memories of Doris Day
Singing
When I was just a little girl
I
Asked my mother
Symbols of a left over faith
Our lady of Fatima
Promised
A sign unto our world
World in thought
World in humor
Encased with Mom's pink curlers
Soul's map for only
25 cents
Enclose a self-addressed envelope
Saturday morning breakfast
Mother of faith
Plastic
Shrine out in the backyard
The grotto of greed
The holograph of hope
Mind
Music
Mother

Calling My Soul

A vision that will unite my being
Ask my creator
Are you there
I become lost

I become as a child
My nightmare
My world
My world
Where are the angelic
Voices
Munch's Bridge
I walk to hold my hands up to my face
I scream
Blink
The echo of an ice cream truck
All flavors I am told
By
A vision
Of a god from an old
Taste the sweetness
Of
Thy own soul
Now scream
Now cry
Now try
Loving all
This is my collect call
To my always loving soul
Just be there for someone
That's all in the taste of life

The Promise

A new soul floated
Down
From the hand
Of
God

Two older souls
Receiving the rarest
Gift
The breath of Life
This moment
Endures
A lifetime
Tears of joy rolling down the cheek
There is a promise
To keep
Child in dreams of musical sleep
Honor
Mother and Father
Shall be the echo
Of
Every heartbeat

The youngest soul
Has much to teach
Remember
Each star
Is
In
One's reach

Listen
Laugh
Weep
For the treasure
Is
A promise
From creation of a new soul
Is our mystery touched
So
Soulfully deep

Angel of Light

Creation spoke
"Lucifer"
Highest Angel
Crowned with the stars
Reflection of all light
Soul of Man
Teach them
Free will

The insight of conscience birth becomes
I Lucifer

I will create
So
The soul of man
Has a state
I will fall from
Grace
Is the story
They will
Write
Speak
Of
My fate

Creation spoke
"Lucifer"
As the tree of life is born
As thoughts are
Another one of you will be asked to be crowned with thorns

Creation spoke
"Jesus"
In a garden the reflection of Lucifer

You will
Fight
Come to know
There is no
Wrong
No
Right

Creation spoke
Creation cried
Creation laughed
Creation breathed

My soul of man
This
Is
A
Gift
Of
Light
Not wrong
Not Right
The gift is your
Soul
Called
Free will
The obedience chosen
By
The light of an angel
Named
"Lucifer"

Our Divine Grace

Who contemplates the name of heaven in all
Our name is one
Give us love for this day
As we may then give love to one another
Enable us to accept ourselves
Bless us with Humility
Enable us to seek with in as onto
Demonstrate for us the act of forgiveness
For we shall inherit the spirit of earth once we understand
this
In knowing ours in all
In the one mind of spirit
So we claim our voice
And
So it is

Puppets of Spirit

Dangling dusty armatures
Some painted with faces of delight
Others painted without life
The dangling crippled wires tangle their lives
My arm moves
Your foot bends
The carved carefulness captures our souls
The life of our puppets
Dances
Our free will to a sacred sound
Out of the voice
All is crafted
Puppets in pain

Dancing and singing
Finally
Amongst heaven's
Rain

ONE DAY

One day I found a wish I made
Fall from the sky of grace
I said
Why or why me

One day I will live to be me
In a land that where all is to be free
This prayer I ask to be

One day I found a wish I made
Raining as my soul cried
I claimed it's just me
Why or why me

One day I know not far away
I will break free
Strokes of colors
They will accept me

If one day I can live honest free
This is a wish for many to see
I will know and believe
I live in a land spoken as the free
Is where you will find me

So until this day we see
A voice of the free
I will always speak of these strokes of colors
To one day be called me

Dancing with Holy Thorns

The glass fell from the sky
Pieces of all sizes
Mirrored memories of all ages
Burning
The umbrella I carry is slashed like a black widow's web
My tears are dark as dirty oil
Why me

God does not answer
How many houses of his holy name must I light a candle in
Kneeling in front of porcelain images of his so-called name
The images of his son carrying the cross for humanity all
around me

I follow his journey until my gaze rests on the resurrection
A stained-glass image of this holy moment
Where is mine I ask
I hear only an echo in this holy house

"Awaken"
I open my eyes to see my home
A HOME
A VISION
A JOURNEY
Not an answer

By myself I can call myself
A survivor or victim
Mercy comes not from heaven
It comes from within

Learn to accept I hear
I lift my head to see the man with thorns on a wooden relic
Suffering

Beyond myself
Beyond himself
For ourselves

A light lifts me out of my earthen vessel
The voice whispers
"Awareness"
I sit back in the darkened cherry pew
I shout
Forgive me to myself
The thorns blossom into wild flowers
The voice is the wind

I awaken
In my soul of a bedroom
The voice whispers
"Life is a journey"
The daily clock awakens me
Morning light dances over my physicalness
Be blessed the voice whispers
And
In returned bless
I answer

The next body of work is a reflection on death and life. I wrote these poems to friends who had lost a loved one and even for myself. I think, as a society, we are taught to fear death. This, I think, is basically because it finalizes our perceived consciousness. What is next? I have no control on my death date. I do, though, have some control on my living life. This is all I have to offer. Death will, in time, accept my offer.

My Mother's Glasses

Her faint eyes reflected an inner world
So serene
Her quiet voice spoke of a divine wisdom
Her hair of grey shimmered with careful thoughts
Her years of age danced within her soul
The music of life still echoed in her voice
I paused
Her love has been a gift
A gift not for me to keep
Rather to share with all that could still hear
A rare lovely heartbeat

CALLED HOME

Her voice still echoes her vibrant life
A woman of truth
A woman of spirit
Quietness
She spoke of words
Long forgotten
Long lived

Her glasses mirrored a life of being
So alive
So lived
Her deep brown eyes at rest
Not hollowed with vein or hate
Now she sleeps amongst the great roots of the tree of life
Her physicalness gone
Her spirit now a dedication of a path she walked
Her soul alive in the heart of creation

Her journey to love others
To teach
Is now my privilege
I aspire to her life

Awakened early on a Saturday morning
By angels singing welcome home
Love has been waiting
Now you are peaceful here
No more aging
Only wisdom
Speaking

My Grace

The ageless clouds of fate passing
I wonder at times
How will I get through life's days of dates
The wind blowing
The leaves on the tree of life
Reflects my song
Of me

All my dreams and memories
Oh these days I see are only a sacred breeze

I ask the sun and moon to raise me so I may see
How beautiful my dreams and visions have come to be
My days were blossoms of color
In the field of life
A sacred thought
I ask my Creator
To bless the world I leave behind
I am flying
I am
Full of my soul's
Grace

The Caregiver

The woman stood there all in white
Her uniform starched and name tag all so bright

Her house echoed the sounds of children's delight
Always homemade cookies in the ceramic jar within our
sight

The woman had a ministry to care for others during the
night
She would be home as the sun mirrored through the window
day's early light

She would start breakfast
The bacon so crisp

The morning highlight would swirl down the stairs to our
nose's delight
This woman I saw much during a certain time of my life

However time passed
Many of her family echoes fell from my sight

And years lost our touch
But memories of her will never escape my grasp

Age awakens my soul to hear the voices from a loving family
She prayed for by her loving touch

In honor of my aunt Virginia who has on angel's wings
flown to the cloud of heaven
Where she is now in the presence of her loved ones
She hears the voice of creation
Saying
A life well lived
And love onto others many times done

The Heart's Gift

His eyes are mirrors of his loving soul
His love is my greatest gift
I know love only by his smile
I feel love in truth by his embrace
I love back
Just by his touch
The beat of his heart
Together
I pray for many years of turning old
So I may say I have been loved
By a soul so near

Love Lost Love Found

The twinkling of a star is a universal reflection
Spiritual love for all
We can never lose love

For it moves as the wind
As we breathe so we love
Love is never forgetting
Our first love
Our last love
Linked in love
A timeless
Precious gift
Love from our creator
Moves all love
Love from the self
Reflects the enduring
A heartbeat
Is a vision
We call life

The next body of work is inspired by various holidays.
Enjoy!

The Soul's Steeple

The angels' voices were all heard in every language
Of this tiny soul
As I listened to the gift they told
My spirit started to shimmer

A shimmer that has always been there
However was darkened with the motion of the coming and
going
Of seasons

My soul now stands on the highest church steeple
My inner breath becomes winter crystals

My eyes are seeing the star that reflects inward
This church steeple is touching the face of heaven

Reflection moves me
My fears melt away into internal light

The angels' voices lift me
Their wings comfort me
All around me
As me
Love

The gift is very simple
The gift is God's love

The gift is living for today
The wrapping paper reflects the moving sky of this winter
day
And all of my days

I stand on this steeple aware of all the other church steeples
Steeples of all sizes reflected against winter's canopy
Of living skies

I see silhouettes of others standing on their own spiral tower
As I am

I know when I want to
My arms will become wings of golden light
In addition, in a winter's breath
Will fly me to the radiant truth
Of thy holy self

And with this I will become an angelic voice
For others
Who only need to listen

Nature's Sanctuary

The whiteness of crystals reflected
A journey back to my childhood
A time that played songs of my playful spirit
I would walk this path with many memories
It had changed
I really don't know even how or why
Maybe it is that I have changed
Amongst this walk in a prayer of snow
The seasons gifted my soul
With the lessons of faith to grow

The Snow Angel

The whiteness of clouds fading into a deep blue sky
Found me standing
Found me lost in distant days
Found me questioning life

My feet would not move up the church's steps
Cold cement covered in snow anchored my feet

I looked up to the old stained glass window
Gabriel grasping the golden trumpet
Announcing the miracle etched into the glass

It has been years since I walked into this church of my youth
I was in awe of the memories that rushed through my soul
A holy waterfall of my creator's grace

Laughter surrounded me
I looked to see children making snow angels
One child had a plastic golden trumpet
Thank you Gabriel
I said with my spirit

I walked up the steps to the church
Years on angel wings going by

This is where I found my faith
Here is where faith found me
On one Christmas Day

No Room in the Inn

Another holiday season
And for what reason
Our world is a battleground

Defining the true god to be found
My mind wakes
Stillness vibrates this soul
Do I always take the word
I am told
I listen to the music of a snowfall
My heart now opened to love called
My faith empowers me to say
There is room in my inn
The breath of my life
Is open to all
So upon me
My creator may call
To speak words of love
I shout from my deepest
Well of pain
Blessing my prayers
As a mourning dove
Soars over all life
This holiest soul
Of sight

The Voice of Three Magi

Follow the star said the magical magi
In the light of its reflection is the promise
The other master of metaphysics spoke
Yet what will this promise bring us
The magical magi spoke
The promise is already here
Within us
Finally the quiet magi spoke raising his hand towards the
star
A simple promise that will change human kind

A simple promise
Yet we need a star to follow
The great star echoed
I am the heart of God
He who believes will see as you do
All three magi rejoiced
We have found life's journey

Winter's Magic

The jolly old elf laughed as white crystals teared in his eyes
of hazel blue
The whiteness of his beard reflected as icicles
The magical colors from the star above
Snowed Christmas Eve

The song of the forest echoed the little valley's church song
of
Joy to the World
The chapel's lighted window glowed of a fire within
The winter spirit of gifts flew above the tree tops
He reached into his earthen bag
And gently graced the earth below
With crystals a glow

Jolly ole St. Nick many call him
This winter spirit is an ageless wise elf
Who will always give insight of thy beautiful self
The moon in fullness
The stars reflected in his eyes
Peace he sung
The wind is his voice
So tonight

Listen
And if you open your heart to pureness
You will hear this gentle winter spirit

Finding Christmas

I found myself asking where is Christmas
As I awoke today
Hearing a deep Midwestern voice of Jack Frost
I went to my Bible
So my inner reflection would be answered
Only Matthew talks about the first Christmas
Oh much credit I give him in describing the event
Yet it did not tell me where to find Christmas
I turned on the television to see the movie
It's a Wonderful Life
Sippin' my Dunkin' Donuts coffee I watched it
I knew surely it would tell me where to find Christmas
It did tell a beautiful message
For no man is a failure who has friends
Yet I felt that wasn't telling me where is Christmas
Looking outside the window
Seeing people going places in their ice-stricken cars
Spinning wheels for a long time on the ice showed
determination
Of celebrating Christmas with loved ones
Yet again this did not answer my question
Even playing holy music throughout the house did not
answer the question
So I thought I should do some cleaning
While spraying Windex on my bedroom mirror
The message came to me
As I wiped the streaks away I saw my own image
The same reflection I see every day

I am Christmas
I thought
I don't have to look for it as a special day
It is everyone's day-to-day reflection
Just pure and simply
Us

The Same Time Next Year

Our paper sheets torn with dates on them
Will fade
All the colors of pens stating Time of meaning will fade
The new whiteness of a year clouding gray
White clouds against blue beginnings will blossom
The brightness of sky turns ultramarine
With tears of joyful reflection
Longer days of scented flowers
And humming bees
Wishes made on the winded butterfly wings
The sensation of our earthly garden being watered
By our soul
Our divine gardener
The leaves changing into an earthen cathedral of colors
We find ourselves again with evergreen delight
A time of saying good-bye
And of hello
To a new us

The Passing of Time

The grandfather clock chimed the voice
Of God
Made from the tree of life's

Olden branches
It reflected every soul
Birth to passing
By the ticking and tocking of the universal theme
Life
The grandfather clock has never stopped
It is the holiest of timekeepers
The wisdom of God bestowed upon its earthly hands
Our soul gathers by the second hand
The coming of a great prophet
Written onto the swinging arm
We bestow our prayers onto this
Time
Time awaits until God winds the great clock
For now we live in time of
Our thought

Dear Father Time

I found myself missing
The laughter and tears of so many old friends
The ones you promised never to forget
BFF
Like olden torn books on the library shelf
Of your mind
So many have moved like a falling star across my sky
Of memory
Where does this lead me
Friendship is the truest reflection of our soul's map
The compass's needle has moved in so many directions
The arch of our sun creates each day
In this thought of time
Where it rises and sets is our home
Even though we still try to hold time

Borrow it
Even cheat it
We still must move long the map
For time is the brushstroke of our creator's expression
Life

Free at Last, Free at Last, Thank God Almighty, Free at Last

The Baptist minister uttered these words
Knowing in his heart it would be more of a prayer
Then
He himself living it
The church bells rang in a raven-sorrowed tear of black
The simple Bible teacher
No longer will teach
His words would become silence
Dying
As a patch of grass
In the garden of living
The holy sun and sacred moon
Will keep rising
Setting beyond memory

A new age would come to the people of this fabled
Land
The lifeless garden would not die
Voices walked by this garden
Ears walked by this garden
Eyes walked by this garden
A thought walked by this garden

Life was reborn
Freedom for all fell onto the hearts of these fabled people

Reflections born of life were the seeds
Planted

Heaven allowed the Baptist minister to rain on to the garden
with his tears
A voice came
A vote by these fabled people
Brought the garden back to the life of so many
The garden blooms
For now we will focus
On
The sacred sun
And
The holy moon